Strategic Argumentation in Parliamentary Debate

Second Edition

Eric

DEDICATION

This book is for people who love to debate.

CONTENTS

ERIC ROBERTSON

1 INTRODUCTION

Purpose of this Text

This text is intended to provide applicable theory and tools to new and experienced debaters. It should give enough background so that anyone who picks it up can grasp the basics of parliamentary debate, and also so that the most experienced debater can use it as a reference. Rather than taking from existing books on debate, this text attempts to explain the tools that are in use NOW, on the current National Parliamentary Debate Association and NPTE circuits, and explain how the best teams are using them in their arguments. This text will explain many of the small details of parliamentary debate, as well as some overall argumentation principles that should be examined when looking at any proposition.

What is Parliamentary Debate?

Parliamentary Debate is a semi-extemporaneous argumentation competition with two people on each team arguing over one topic. The debaters do not know the topic until **twenty minutes** before the round starts, and topics are often drawn from current events but also may be from general subject areas. Throughout this text Parliamentary Debate will often be referred to as *Parli* in order to get the reader accustomed to the speech patterns of many debaters.

The team who supports the topic is known as the **Government**, and the team who opposes the topic is known as the **Opposition**. The first speaker on the Government Team is known as the Prime Minister, and the second speaker on the Government Team is know as the Member of Government. On the Opposition, the first speaker is known as the Leader of Opposition, and the second speaker is known as the Member of Opposition. Each side has three speeches to make their case, and the order is as follows:

Prime Minister Constructive (7 Minutes)
Leader of Opposition Constructive (8 Minutes)
Member of Government Constructive (8 Minutes)
Member of Opposition Constructive (8 Minutes)
Leader of Opposition Rebuttal (4 minutes)
Prime Minister Rebuttal (5 Minutes)

The term **constructive** refers to the fact that in the first four speeches debaters are still able to build their case. What this means is that they can bring in new arguments in these speeches, although some debaters contest that certain arguments are not fair to discuss later on in the constructives since they take too much time to respond to and need to be addressed early on. The two speeches at the end of the debate are the **rebuttals**. These two speeches are intended to tie the entire debate together, and to clarify which issues each team believes they are winning.

Speech Interruptions

There are three ways that debaters can interrupt the speech of their opponent. They are as follows:

Points of Information
Points of Order
Points of Personal Privilege
Points of Information

Points of Information, also known as POI's, are the most common interruption in parliamentary debate. They can only be brought up during the constructive speeches, and are generally used to clarify a point or as a form of cross-examination. They are raised by standing up or raising one's hand, and the debater asking the point of information needs to wait for the speaker to recognize him or her before speaking. Usually POI's are no longer than five seconds, and debaters are generally only allowed to ask one question at a time. Points of information cannot be used during **protected time**, which occurs *before the first minute and after the last minute of the first four constructive speeches*. The judge usually signals that protected time is over or has begun by slapping his or her hand on a table or desk.

Points of Order

In the rebuttals, new arguments are not allowed. If a new argument is brought into a rebuttal, the team listening to the argument has the right to stand up and call a Point of Order. When this happens, the judge stops the time, and listens to the complaint regarding which argument is new. After that, the team who was speaking is able to respond and discuss whether or not they disagree with the Point of Order. Once each team has commented on the Point of Order, the judge rules whether or not he or she will allow the argument.

Points of Personal Privilege

The third type of interruption is a Point of Personal Privilege. This is reserved for teams that feel they are being attacked or insulted in an unnecessary or offensive way. Points of Personal Privilege are very rare and should only be used in serious situations of harassment.

Topics

The topic, also known as the resolution, is announced 20 minutes before the debate starts. Generally students should prepare for 15 minutes, and 5 minutes should be allotted for walking to the room. In parliamentary debate, topics are usually interpreted as a claim of fact, claim of value, or claim of policy. The topics are often very vague, so it is the role of the government team to explain how they are interpreting the resolution. This is often referred to *resolutional analysis*. For example, with a topic of "This house should fix it," the government team has many options as to how they would like to create their case in support of this topic. They may interpret this topic in a way that argues for the building of more animal hospitals, because currently in the status quo there aren't enough. Their resolutional analysis would sound something like this "We, the government, are going to define this house as the California State Government, we are going to define should as implying action, and we are interpreting fix it as to fix the current lack of animal hospitals for stray dogs."

Notice in the example how some words are defined one at a time, and some are defined as a group. Either is acceptable, as long as it makes sense. In other cases, topics may be much more specific, such as "This house should increase sanctions on Iran." This topic should still be defined, and would sound something like this, "This house is defined as the United States, should implies action, and increase sanctions on Iran means to add on to the pre-existing penalties the US currently imposes on Iran. Iran is the Middle Eastern Country of Iran." Since topics like this are not necessarily vague and the Government team is defining the words in the most common way possible, often times teams will simply say, "We are going to take the resolution at face value, any questions?" At this time, the Opposition Team could interrupt (by standing silently) with a point of information to clarify anything they may not completely believe to be clear. Also, in a claim of policy, some teams will define the resolution through the plan text. Since the topic implies action, this type of advocacy illustrates support of the resolution by demonstrating an action that exemplifies the claim. Therefore, in this method of defining, the plan is the embodiment of the definitions. This subject is discussed in further detail in the counterplan section.

There are different types of resolutions, and each has a different approach that debaters need to understand when creating their case. The three types of claims are: claims of fact, claims of policy, or claims of value.

Claims of Fact

Claims of fact are rarely debated in senior levels of Parliamentary Debate today. There are a few reasons for this. First, since claims of fact usually have a definitive answer of being true or false, generally they are less popular. Also, since parliamentary debaters cannot bring in evidence to a round, the accuracy of facts is always somewhat in question. Students usually don't benefit with the same level of education since there is generally less clash over the issue. However, since many coaches and judges do believe that there are three distinct types of resolutions, claims of fact will be discussed.

Claims of fact look at a relationship between two things, or the existence of something in the past, present or future. Examples of these are as follows:

Functional Factual Claims
Assert that something causes something else. Functional is referring to an object being acted upon to cause a result.

Example: The debater made his team win the tournament.

In this example the relationship between the debater and his effect on the tournament the issue that would be debated.

Temporal Factual Claims
Asserts that something happened, is happening, or will happen. Temporal is referring to time.
<u>Past</u>
George W. Bush ruined America.

<u>Present</u>
Millions of Americans are unemployed.

<u>Future</u>
Flying cars will change everything we know about transportation.

Each of the above three examples are claims of fact. Notice how the temporal claim of fact that looks at future relationships has not yet happened, but the aspect of "changing everything" would be considered a fact that could be argued.

Claims of Value

Claims of Value are statements that garner their

support or opposition from abstract concepts. Examples of a value would include concepts like freedom, justice, wealth, education, liberty, and health. Notice how these are beliefs that can be used to justify certain behaviors. For example, I am going to school because I want to further my education. Education is not something tangible that one receives; rather, it is a state that one embodies and demonstrates through educated behaviors. A good way to tell if something actually is considered to be a value is to fill in the blank in the following sentence. "I live my life for _____." There are a few exceptions, but generally speaking, this can be an easy way for beginners to understand whether or not something would be considered a value. The reason that this test makes sense is because when saying that you live your life for something, you are showing a value that you find important that drives your behaviors. There are a few different types of value resolutions. The first is the privileging value. This shows one particular concept over another. For example,

The rights of the individual are more important than the rights of the community.
Or
Wine is better than beer.

The second type of value resolution is the above all others value. For example:

Dogs are the best type of animal.

The difference between the two is small, because the second sentence could be rewritten as "Dogs are better than all other types of animals," and you would have the same meaning, but for our purposes this delineation is important because of the specific arguments that are generated by having more than one group in comparison.

Claims of Policy

Claims of policy are statements that are advocating some sort of change to the status quo. In other words, they imply that there needs to be some kind of action to fix a problem. For example;

This house should stop the press.
Or
The United States Federal Government should significantly increase renewable energy.

Here we have an abstract topic and a concrete topic. However, notice how each is prompting the debater to act. This house/the USFG should actually do something; in this case, they should stop the press or increase renewable energy. This is the most popular type of claim on the competitive circuit today and is discussed in much greater depth later on in the text.

Summary

This chapter covered a significant amount of information. It discussed speaker names, speech times, overall debate format, and different types of resolutions. The next chapter will go more in depth regarding each resolution and procedures for case construction.

2 TOPICS AND INTERPRETATIONS

Introduction of Criterion

In the last chapter we discussed resolutional analysis and the process of defining words that may be ambiguous. Directly after this step, the Prime Minister must provide the judge with a way to evaluate the arguments presented in the round. This is known as a **criterion**. While the following examples are not necessarily the best, they are by far the most common in Parliamentary Debate today.

Fact Cases

Preponderance of Evidence- Whoever has the most and best evidence wins.

Think of a fact case like a court case. Our resolution can be: Joe committed murder (In this example, you are Joe). If you are on trial, the prosecution will present as many facts as possible to show that you are guilty. They will show how you were at the scene of the crime, how you had fingerprints on the murder weapon, and so on. If they show 15 pieces of evidence that link you to the crime, and your defense attorney can only show one piece of evidence, let's say a testimony from your best friend saying that you were at their house on the other side of town, odds are you will get convicted.

Problems with this criterion: Who is to say which piece of evidence is better? For our example, let's say that a DNA test showed that the blood on the murder weapon wasn't yours. Wouldn't that one piece of evidence be strong enough to cast serious doubt into the mind of the jury, even though there were 14 other pieces introduced by the prosecution? The concept of counting pieces of evidence, or in the case of debate, the number of contentions, doesn't really make too much sense when some evidence is much better than others. This forces judges to weigh out the quality of your evidence through their own personal lens, which often can make decisions both challenging for the judge and hard for debaters to understand. Also, any times examples are present with fairly equal strength on each side, which forces judges to intervene to make a decision.

Value Cases

On Balance- The government team should win if they can provide more and better examples that support their interpretation of the topic.

This should be thought of as a scale, where certain pieces of evidence can weigh more than others, and whoever has the most and best arguments should win.

Problems with this criterion: Very subjective. This is similar to the preponderance of evidence criterion, except it is used in value cases. It is in essence saying-vote for the team with the best arguments, which might as well have not been said. The judge knows they are going to vote for the team with the best arguments. This is a given. It can often force judges to weigh apples against oranges, so they are forced to draw upon their own personal beliefs and biases, which is often problematic. Since certain values resonate with some judges more than others, audience analysis is extremely important when presenting these arguments.

Policy Case

Net Benefits- The government team should win if the pros of the plan outweigh the costs of not doing the plan. Basically this comes down to looking at what happens when the problem is solved and what impacts the advantages will create and weighing that against the negative consequences of the plan.

Problems with this criterion: Very vague. It forces judges to weigh out impacts on all levels. Should a judge vote for a plan that kills 100,000 people to save 101,000 people? If the Opposition Team can't make a compelling argument why that 101,000 people won't die without the passage of the plan, then in theory, it is better to do the plan than to not do the plan. While this may sound like a criterion that makes sense at first, the philosophy that backs it can be used to justify things like torture and medical testing on humans.

So far we have discussed how to identify the different types of claims, resolutional analysis, and criterion. These are the first things that are heard out of the mouth of a debater on the Government. In the next chapter, we will discuss specific case structures and provide examples for each type of claim.

3 GOVERNMENT CASE STRUCTURES

This chapter is intended to be a reference for case construction. The cases here are not the only way to construct an argument, however, they are currently the most common.

At the very beginning of a debate, there should be a brief and compelling introduction. This can include a quote, analysis, or a story. Keep it short and simple. Also, quickly thank the judges, your partner, and your opponent for being there. Again, short and simple.

Fact Cases

One of the most important things to keep in mind is that fact cases don't require impacts. What this means is that when presenting contentions in a fact case, the argument needs to describe the situation, and sometimes, its relationship to the other object in the resolution. Fact cases do not need to tell us why these issues are important, rather, their goal is to convince us that they *exist* and truly represent an example of support for the resolution.

Fact Case Format

Introductory Remarks
State topic and that your team supports it
Interpretation of topic as fact, value, or policy
Resolutional Analysis
Criterion
Contention 1 (1-3 word title)
Provide an example of something that supports the resolution
Link- Specifically show how this relates to the resolution

Contention 2 (1-3 word title)
Provide an example of something that supports the resolution
Link- Specifically show how this relates to the resolution

Contention 3 (1-3 word title)
Provide an example of something that supports the resolution
Link- Specifically show how this relates to the resolution

Contention 4 (1-3 word title)
Provide an example of something that supports the resolution
Link- Specifically show how this relates to the resolution

Contention 5 (1-3 word title)
Provide an example of something that supports the resolution
Link- Specifically show how this relates to the resolution

Final Closing remarks, reaffirming support of the resolution

Review

Notice how the example here provided five contentions. It is recommended to have between three and five contentions in a fact case; however, there is no set requirement. The most important consideration is the quality of the facts that you will be discussing.

The following is an example of a fact case, written as if it were created during a 15-minute prep time. Since cases are almost never written out in complete sentences, these examples will attempt to mirror what is actually created.

Example Fact Prime Minister Constructive

Topic: America is too obsessed with celebrities (topic taken from PSCFA Warm Up, 2008)

Introduction
    Discuss North Korean threats of violence against the US. Juxtapose against news coverage domination of recent celebrity deaths (Michael Jackson)
    Support Resolution
    Criterion- Preponderance of Evidence (explain)

Contention 1 Celebrity Deaths Overshadow News
    Discuss Farah Faucet, MJ, Billy Mays and North Korea.
    Link- Our lives are in danger but because America is too obsessed with celebrities we don't hear about more important news

Contention 2 Dangerous
    Discuss paparazzi, Princess Diana Death,

Link- Because of the unhealthy obsession with celebrities, their lives are in danger

Contention 3 Bad role models
Chris Brown and Rianna domestic abuse. Other celebs with alcohol problems, rehab, etc.
Link- The over-intrusive nature of our relationship into the personal lives of these people shows how we are too obsessed with them.

For all of these facts, we stand in strong support of the resolution: America is too obsessed with celebrities.

Value Cases

Value cases are a bit more tricky than fact cases, simply because there are multiple ways to construct them. The first style discussed here looks at a single value and attempts to tailor the arguments around that specific concept. It starts out very similar to a fact case, with the largest difference being the evaluative portion of the argument, seen here as the impact. The impact tells us why we should care and how the issue is important.
Value Case Format 1

Introduction
State the topic and that your team supports it
Resolutional analysis
State that this will be a value case
State the value and why you believe it is important
Criterion

Contention 1
Status Quo- Describe a situation or scenario
Link- Show a link to the resolution
Impact- Explain why it is important and how it

upholds the value

    Contention 2
    Status Quo
    Link
    Impact

    Contention 3
    Status Quo
    Link
    Impact

    Closing Remarks

Similar to a fact case, this should have roughly three to five contentions, although there is no set number. There is some controversy over whether or not a single value should be used in a value case. While some believe that this provides clarity that can focus the debate on one particular issue, others believe that values are so intertwined with each other that the government team is setting up an impossible burden. For example, if the government team were to use the value of love, critics argue that they would have the burden to show how all of the contentions illustrate love more than they illustrate any other value. So if the Opposition Team were to show how these contentions illustrate, say, compassion, more so than love, then the government team is not meeting the burden that they themselves set up.

The second format presented here is more open-ended, and allows for more flexibility in the presentation of the case. It can include more than one value to justify the resolution, but this format should limit each contention to one specific value.

Value Case Format 2

Introduction
Statement in support of the resolution
Resolutional analysis
Criterion

Contention 1
Status Quo
Link explaining the tie to the topic
Impact that illustrates the value at hand and why it is
important in this scenario

Contention 2
Status Quo
Link explaining the tie to the topic
Impact that illustrates the value at hand and why it is
important in this scenario

Contention 3
Status Quo
Link explaining the tie to the topic
Impact that illustrates the value at hand and why it is
important in this scenario

Contention 4
Status Quo
Link explaining the tie to the topic
Impact that illustrates the value at hand and why it is
important in this scenario

Contention 5
Status Quo
Link explaining the tie to the topic

Impact that illustrates the value at hand and why it is important in this scenario

Policy Cases

By far the most popular of all claim interpretations at the moment is a claim of policy. As discussed in the previous chapter, this type of claim advocates change in the status quo. There are two main formats for this type of debate, and while neither is best, comparative advantages is used much more at the senior levels. The first format is usually referred to as "stock issues." When looked at through this lens, the government team believes that its responsibility is to identify a significant problem, show how that problem is not going away, propose a plan, show how that plan solves the problem, and then also discuss additional added benefits of the plan.

Policy Case- Stock Issues Format

Introduction
Resolutional Analysis
Criterion

Harms (also known as significance)- Discuss the problem that needs to be solved. The government team has the burden to solve any problem that they introduce in this section. It is wise to only have one large harm here.

Inherency- This discusses how the problem will not go away. It illustrates the cause for the harm, and why it is going to continue to exist in the status quo unless plan is enacted.

Plan Text- This brief section describes exactly what the

plan will do in order to solve for the harm.

Agency- This discusses the group of people who will enact the plan

Mandate- This is the exact thing that will be done. Sometimes teams include this first as a substitute for plan text, as they are very similar. Be sure to include when it will be passed as well as what the plan entails.

Enforcement- This section explains how the plan will be implemented.

Funding- This section discusses how the plan will be paid for. Often times debaters will use the term "normal means," for plans that are not particularly expensive, or that are usually covered in the general budgets allotted for their agency.

Solvency- This provides analysis and examples that explain how the plan will actually solve for the problem. Did it work in another similar instance? Does it make intuitive sense that by implementing the plan the inherency will no longer exist therefore decreasing the harm?

Advantages- Also known as unique advantages, this section discusses the "bonuses" that will also come along with the plan. Will it set a precedent that will help other worthy causes? Will the revenue created by the plan fund something else? Here you are able to look down the road at all of the things that passing a plan will influence, directly or indirectly, and make arguments that show how the plan is good in many ways. There can be as many advantages as the government team has time for, however, these are not the main concern of the plan, therefore, if the plan doesn't solve, then these arguments don't matter.

The following is an example of an outline that would be created in the 15 minutes of prep time for a policy resolution using the stock issues format.

Sample Policy Stock Issues Case

Intro- Marijuana brings in over 13 billion dollars per year to California's economy which is untaxed, unregulated, and unsafe.

Support Resolution- TH should legalize it

TH= The state of California

Should= implies action

Legalize it= pass legislation to make marijuana legal in the state of California Details will be provided in plan.

Harms-

CA Economy

State workers I O U's

Currently 21.3 billion dollar budget deficit

Approaching 10% unemployment

Inherency

This budget will continue to be in debt as long as there is not enough money coming in. Marijuana is a significant potential source of income for the State of California, and it will be a great start to helping fix this monumental problem.

Plan

Mandate: The state government of California will legalize marijuana in all forms for individuals 21 years of age or older.

Enforcement: Quality will be enforced by the FDA and the Bureau of Alcohol, Tobacco and Firearms will control distribution.

Timeframe- Immediately

Funding- through normal means, and will generate

significant tax revenue.

Solvency
Through the taxation of marijuana millions and over time, billions of dollars of tax revenues will go directly to the government. Not only that, but the entire enterprise will generate movement in the economy which will lead to more overall consumption. The taxation on cigarettes produces over 15 billion dollars each year, and many analysts say that the tax on marijuana would create much more demand than cigarettes.

Unique Advantages

UA 1 Education
Status Quo- Currently, due to a massive budget shortfall, many teachers have been laid off. Over 25,000 have been laid off this year.

Link- By passing plan, these jobs could be saved.

Impact- More teachers means higher quality education, both due to lower class sizes and better quality instruction. With better education we see less drop outs in high school, and eventually the high correlation between education and income will help California and the world increase the standard of living and quality of life.

UA 2 Organized Crime
Status Quo- Currently because marijuana is illegal, criminals are the ones who control the distribution. Because of this, violence over illegal drugs continues to kill innocent victims, as well as increase gang activities.

Link- By passing plan, the criminals who control marijuana will no longer have their source of income from this illegal drug.

Impact- There are a variety of different situations that could arise out of this. One, is that these criminals who are experts in the growth and selling of marijuana would be able to escape a life of crime and would be able to participate in the marijuana trade legally. Another impact that would come out of plan passing is that gang violence could go down, which would lead to a lowering of rape, murder, and assault.

UA 3 Hemp

Status Quo- Currently since all forms of marijuana are illegal, hemp cannot be produced. Hemp is a form of marijuana that does not contain enough THC to get someone high, but it can be used for renewable energy as well as very strong rope.

Link- By legalizing marijuana, all hemp products would be able to be grown in CA.

Impact- This could offset some of our nations dependence on foreign oil, as well as add to the economy. Discuss how any reduction in foreign oil is good.

Policy Case- Comparative Advantages Format

The other format for policy cases is known as comparative advantages. This format is the most commonly used on the national level, and has become the standard in most senior level debates. The main difference is "harms" are not discussed, and the case moves quickly into the plan. In addition, the advantages are tied to the solvency and are weighed more heavily than unique advantages in the stock issues format. The format outline is as follows:

Introduction
Resolutional Analysis
Criterion

Background- Here the government briefly discusses the current situation that exists in the status quo. It is similar to harms in the stock issues format, however, it can be more holistic and it not only discusses the problem but the surrounding events that are causing the situation to need some sort of plan.

PLAN- After the background, the plan is presented. Same format as stock issues:

Plan text- This brief section describes exactly what the plan will do in order to solve for the harm.

Agency- This discusses the group of people who will enact the plan

Mandate- This is the exact thing that will be done. Sometimes teams include this first as a substitute for plan text, as they are very similar. Be sure to include when it will be passed as well as what the plan entails.

Enforcement- This section explains how the plan will be implemented.

Funding- This section discusses how the plan will be paid for. Often times debaters will use the term "normal means," for plans that are not particularly expensive, or that are usually covered in the general budgets allotted for their agency.

Advantage 1 (3-5 word title of advantage)

Status Quo- Discuss a situation that currently exists that does not include the plan

Link- Tie this situation to a feature that exists in the current status quo, such as a law, attitude, etc.

Solvency- Show how plan changes the status quo either by removing some type of barrier or adding something new, and discuss how it fulfills the resolution.

Impact- Discuss in depth why this is important and why your judge should care.

While there are some similarities, the main differences are that the background is usually discussed for a shorter period of time than the harms, and advantages are presented in a way that is more closely tied to the solvency and it carries more weight. Debaters usually include roughly 3-5 advantages, although there is no set rule.

Comparative Advantages Sample Case

Using the same resolution, here is an example of comparative advantages

Intro- Marijuana brings in over 13 billion dollars per year to California's economy which is untaxed, unregulated, and unsafe.

Support Resolution- TH Should legalize it

TH= The state of California

Should implies action

Legalize it= pass legislation to make marijuana legal in the state of California Details will be provided in plan.

Background- The state of California is in very bad shape. State workers I O U's

Currently 21.3 billion dollar budget deficit

Approaching 10% unemployment. This is mainly due to the lack of tax revenue coming in to the state government. We must find a way to increase this revenue, or else the state government could collapse as we know it. Therefore we propose the following plan.

Plan

Mandate: The state government of California will legalize marijuana in all forms for individuals 21 years of age or older.

Enforcement: Quality will be enforced by the FDA

and the Bureau of Alcohol, Tobacco and Firearms will control distribution.

Timeframe- Immediately

Funding will be through normal means, and will generate significant tax revenue.

Advantages

Advantage 1 Education

Status Quo- Currently, due to a massive budget shortfall, many teachers have been laid off. Over 25,000 have been laid off this year.

Link- By passing plan, these jobs could be saved because the budget shortfall would be fixed.

Solvency- The legalization of marijuana would make a positive change by allowing these teachers to keep their jobs.

Impact- More teachers allows for higher quality education, both due to lower class sizes and better quality instruction. With better education we see less drop outs in high school, and eventually the high correlation between education and income will help California and the world increase the standard of living and quality of life.

Advantage 2 Organized Crime

Status Quo- Currently because marijuana is illegal, criminals are the ones who control the distribution. Because of this, violence over illegal drugs continues to kill innocent victims, as well as increase gang activities.

Link- By passing plan, the criminals who control marijuana will no longer have their source of income from this illegal drug.

Solvency- The legalization of marijuana will then make the streets safer and lower crime in many areas.

Impact- There are a variety of different situations that could arise out of this. One, is that these criminals who are experts in the growth and selling of marijuana would be able to escape a life of crime and would be able to participate in the marijuana trade legally. Another impact that would come out of plan passing is that gang violence could go down, which would lead to a lowering of rape, murder, and assault.

So for all of these reasons we strongly believe that the California State Government should legalize marijuana.

Differences Between the Two Formats

Notice that both cases are doing the same thing. They are both demonstrating that there is a problem that needs to be fixed with a plan. The comparative advantages format moves a little bit faster than the stock issues format. Some proponents of the stock issues format will provide multiple harms early on in the case and then multiple solvency points that demonstrate how the plan solves for each harm. One of the issues with this is that the government team places themselves at a disadvantage by providing multiple harms, since the burden of the government team is to solve for the harms. If they don't solve for one out of their three harms, they may lose the debate. While using the similar arguments in the comparative advantages format, the government will only have to solve for the main issue discussed in the background, and if one of their advantages is defeated they can still win the debate. This is likely one of the main reasons that at the senior levels the comparative advantages format is much more popular than the stock issues format.

4 OPPOSITION STRATEGIES

Now that we have discussed the formats for the government team, let's take a look at some common strategies that the opposition can use to create arguments. If you were thinking to yourself, "But if they can interpret the resolution any way they want, how can the Opposition Team possibly prepare during prep time without knowing their interpretations?" Great question. There are two main ways to prepare against this strategic advantage of the government definitions. The first is to predict. In almost all cases with only a few exceptions, there are probably only a total of three or four potential interpretations for any topic. In many cases where the resolution is very straight forward, it is easy to predict the direction the government team is going to go. The job of the Opposition Team is to prepare arguments against the *possibilities* that the government team could use. This is rhetoric at its finest. Aristotle said, "Rhetoric may be defined as the faculty of observing in any given case the available means of persuasion." This is exactly what the opposition needs to do. Find the available means of persuasion, and then create arguments to oppose the potential government cases.

The second way to prepare against arguments is to limit the government team. There are only a certain number of interpretations that are fair to the opposition. For example, if the resolution were " This house should fix the locks," it would be fair to say that the government team shouldn't be discussing fixing the locks on their dad's storage shed. So, in essence, the opposition prepares by looking at a topic and saying, okay, these interpretations are legitimate, and I will prepare for them, and these are not, so I will create arguments that prepare to say why we shouldn't have to debate poor interpretations. There are many ways to construct opposition arguments, and the most common are listed and discussed in this chapter. They include: topicality, direct refutation, counter contentions, disadvantages, counterplans, Kritiks, and Spec/Vagueness Arguments.

Topicality

In the previous chapter, resolutional analysis was discussed as a way for the government to define the topic. Debaters will often work with the resolution as a way to provide them a strategic advantage. In other words, if the government team can provide a legitimate interpretation that the Opposition Team is not ready for, they are more likely to win the debate. However, creative interpretations can sometimes be unrealistic and unfair for the Opposition Team to debate. If you are on the opposition side in a debate, and the government team defines the topic in a way that you feel is unfair, the correct way to respond is with a topicality argument.

A topicality argument looks like this:

Interpretation
Violation
Standards
Voting Issue

The **interpretation** portion simply says that this is what we believe that this word or these words would have been in order to be fair. Usually the reasons why your interpretation is best are discussed in the standards.

The **violation** compares your interpretation to the definitions provided by the Government. In other words, you think it should be X; their interpretation was Y, so notice that X and Y are very different.

The **standards** are arguably the most important portion of the topicality position. Basically what standards include are certain rules or concepts that people agree that fair definitions should contain.

Field Context- Certain topic areas have jargon and specified language that are unique to their subject. The argument here is that the interpretation of the topic should be consistent with the language that individuals in that field are using. Fields with their own linguistic parameters such as science and academia are preferable because they provide clear context-specific definitions.

Literature- This standard looks at things that are published as a reason for an interpretation. For example, this was in the New York Times the last five days in a row, and no one is talking about your interpretation. The literature supports our interpretation.

Ground- This standard argues that each side should

have relatively equal access to arguments on each side. By defining the resolution in a way that is completely unpredictable and random, the Opposition Team is unable to prepare good arguments during prep time. Be sure to articulate ground loss by reading a portion of some of the arguments that are now irrelevant. Otherwise, the government team will accuse your team of unarticulated ground loss, or in other words, that you are making it up that you have great arguments that you can't use.

Common Usage- Man on the street interpretation. This standard argues that the most common interpretation is best, or at least that the way that the government team defined the resolution is inherently uncommon.

Grammar- Since topics are generally read out loud, this is a very difficult standard to apply in parliamentary debate. The most common way it is used is when the topic specifically has a word that includes an "s," which makes one or more of the definable terms plural. If the word should be plural and the government team defines it in a singular way, then they are not topical.

Education- This is a fairly common standard although it is pretty bad. This can be run in conjunction with ground, if the opposition argues that the clash of arguments, meaning the head to head discussion of points, is the most educational activity possible. The loss of clash that has resulted due the randomness of definitions has lead to a loss in education. This standard is very challenging to win on because it is nearly impossible to define what is educational and what is not.

Predictability- This standard usually should not be run alone, and commonly is run with ground. It basically says that there were only a few reasonable interpretations that the Opposition Team could predict to make the debate fair. The government team defined it in an unpredictable way, therefore it is not fair for the opposition.

<u>Framers Intent</u>- This is probably the least effective of all commonly used topicality arguments. Debaters who use this standard explain that the person who created the topic believed it was supposed to be interpreted in a certain way. There are a few reasons why this is a poor standard. First of all, if any of the debaters know the topics and their justifications beforehand, that is a form of cheating. Second, it doesn't really matter what the framer intended. If it is vague and the rules allow for interpretation, then the original intent is irrelevant. The only time that this standard is reasonable is in tournaments that have certain topic areas. For example, Point Loma Nazarene University hosts a tournament that usually provides topic areas. One of the topic areas was drawn from Barack Obama's inauguration speech. This was announced beforehand, therefore it is reasonable that the topic should be interpreted in a way that has something to do with US Federal Government policies and values.

<u>Brightline</u>- Does our definition explain a topic to provide specific parameters from which the judge can understand topicality? For example, if the resolution is "This house should significantly reduce the number of inmates in federal prison," and the government team defines significantly as "a major reduction," then the Opposition Team has an opportunity to provide a better definition. Let's say that the Opposition Team was able to cite in recent literature (using brightline in conjunction with the literature standard) and define significantly as 20%. The Opposition Team would then argue that the government team is lowering the number of inmates less than 20%, and are therefore not topical. On the government side, the definition is very vague, on the opposition side, the definition provides a clear delineation

of what is significant and what is not. 20% is significant, 19% is not. Therefore the government team must lower the number of inmates by 20% or more. In cases like this, the brightline standard clarifies a government definition, while simultaneously illustrating how the government is not meeting the burden set forth by the better definition.

The fourth component of topicality involves explaining to your judge why topicality is a **voting issue**. Other arguments are weighted against each other, but the Opposition Team should argue that since definitions are the foundation for all arguments and all potential cases, they should be considered first. This concept is known as *a priori*, literally translated as "from the former." In other words, it comes before the case and is a foundational necessity to create a legitimate debate. Debaters should mention a priori in this section. Although a priori is not actually a voter, it should be discussed since it is a method of explanation as to why topicality should be its own independent reason to vote for the opposition. The most common voting issues include:

Jurisdiction- The concept here is that the judge is responsible for voting on a case that has something to do with the resolution. If the government team is not arguing for a reasonable interpretation of the resolution, then the judge does not have the authority to vote for it. Since the judge is locked out of making a decision on the debate because of a violation committed by the government team, they are then obligated to vote for the Opposition Team.

Fairness- This is probably the strongest argument to make as a voting issue in topicality. If the government team has constructed a case that is fundamentally unfair to the Opposition Team, then the judge is obligated to vote them down. Debaters agree that there should be at least some level of fairness when preparing for a case, and when the government team denies the Opposition Team reasonable arguments by defining them out of the round, it is the duty of the judge to vote against them. So if the judge believes the opposition has made a convincing argument that the definitions used by the government are unfair, then the government team should lose the debate based upon this fact.

Direct Refutation (Also known as on-case, also known as Four-Point Refutation)

This type of argument on the opposition side is direct clash with the government. The format is as follows:

Identify the Argument: In their _____, they said: Here you are locating their argument and you are briefly recapping what they said. Remember not to linger too long here; your job is merely to show the judge exactly what argument you are responding to, not to re-argue the point for your opponent.

Preview your Argument: This section discusses what you are going to do. It often starts with "we are going to show that ..."

Data and Reasoning: Here you are providing your counter argument. You can attempt this with a few different techniques, whether it is because it is not empirically proven, reasoning supports a different perspective, data contradicts your opponents point, or any other way that you think could be justification that their argument should not stand. This is also a great place to provide counter examples that directly disprove the point made by your opponent.

Impact: The main idea here to provide weight to your argument. You need to elaborate on why this point matters, both in the debate round and within the actual scenario being discussed.

For example, let's say that the resolution was "Cats are better than dogs." The Government Team has provided an argument that sounds something like this:

Contention 1: Cats are the smartest animals around. They know when to conserve energy so that when they need to attack their prey, they have reserves to make sudden strikes. This allows them to feed their family and keep them safe.

A response to this argument using **four-point refutation** would look something like this:

In their first contention, they discussed how cats are the smartest animals around because they can conserve energy. However, we disagree, and we will show you that the ability to conserve energy doesn't necessarily make a creature smart. We believe that cats are lazy and do the minimal amount necessary just to survive. We believe that if cats used more energy, they could produce more and keep their families even safer. The impact here is that since cat's conserve energy, it actually makes their families less safe because they could be using their energy in many other ways and don't need to be conserving it.

This structure works on both the government and the opposition side. It can be used to directly respond to ANY argument.

While topicality and 4-point refutation can be applied to any type of resolution (fact, value, or policy), there are arguments that only should be used with specific topic interpretations.

Opposition Fact Cases

Counter Contentions

Debaters who use this strategy are creating the same contentions that the government created, only on the other side of the issue. The format looks like this:

Counter Contention 1 (1-3 word title)

Provide an example of something that opposes the resolution

Link- Specifically show how this relates to the opposition of the resolution

Counter Contention 2 (1-3 word title)

Provide an example of something that opposes the resolution

Link- Specifically show how this relates to the opposition of the resolution

Counter Contention 3 (1-3 word title)

Provide an example of something that opposes the resolution

Link- Specifically show how this relates to the opposition of the resolution

Does this look familiar? It should. Fact cases are very similar in their structure. The government is providing facts that illustrate examples of support for the resolution; the opposition is presenting facts that oppose the resolution. Notice that there is no resolutional analysis in this example, because it is not the burden of the Opposition Team to provide definitions. The only reasons that the opposition would want to discuss definitions is to raise a topicality argument or to simply agree and acknowledge them.

The most common arguments in a fact case are 4-point refutation and counter contentions. The next most common argument would be topicality, followed by kritiks. We will discuss kritiks later on in this chapter.

Opposition Value Cases

Since the format of a government value case is usually very similar to a fact case, it makes sense that the opposition arguments are fairly similar as well. These arguments are also called counter contentions. The format is as follows:

Counter Contention 1
Status quo illustrating an example that is counter to the resolution
Link explaining how this example disproves the value
Impact that argues why this value is important in this scenario

Counter Contention 2
Status quo illustrating an example that is counter to the resolution
Link explaining how this example disproves the value
Impact that argues why this value is important in this scenario

Counter Contention 3
Status quo illustrating an example that is counter to the resolution
Link explaining how this example disproves the value
Impact that argues why this value is important in this scenario

Remember, the values argued by the Government Team are usually not contestable unless the opposition can somehow prove that they are not values at all. Because of this, these counter contentions can be used against both formats presented in the government section.

Also notice that in both fact and value counter contentions, the examples only include three counter contentions. This is because generally it is not necessary to prep too much more than this since the opposition still has the burden to respond to the contentions brought up by the Government Team. Even if the government argues three contentions, and the opposition argues three counter contentions and responds to everything the government said, it is still challenging to get all of this in during an eight-minute speech.

Opposition Policy Cases

The most common arguments presented in opposition policy cases are disadvantages. Basically a disadvantage explains the negative things that implementing the government plan will cause. It is formatted as follows:

Disadvantage 1- Brief 1-3 word title
Status Quo- Here you explain a situation that currently exists

Link- This section discusses the fact that the plan will influence or change that situation.

Internal Link- This section discusses how the change will lead to the changing of other important issues.

Impact- This section is generally considered the most important; it is where you discuss how this is going to be negative. This section is where you discuss who will be hurt, how badly, why that hurt is bad, and really explain the horrible things that will occur because of the government plan.

Some students have trouble with the internal link

section of this argument, and often times you will see this argument as follows:

Disadvantage 1- Brief 1-3 word title
Status Quo- Describe a situation that currently exists
Link- Describe how the government plan is going to change the situation
Impact- This section is where you discuss who will be hurt, how badly, why that hurt is bad, and really explain the horrible things that will occur because of the government plan.

The main difference between the two is that the internal link describes in more detail how the plan will change the status quo. It is a deeper level of analysis than the second format, although, the second format is often times equally persuasive and easier to use.

There is another format that labels the status quo as the term "uniqueness." The reasoning behind this is to illustrate that the situation discussed will be uniquely effected by the government plan, and it will not lead to the impacts without their specific advocacy. The format is as follows:

Uniqueness- Discuss a situation that will remain unchanged without the government plan.
Link- Explain how the government plan will change the situation.
Internal Link- Discuss how this change will lead to changes in other important areas.
Impact- Elaborate on all of the negative consequences of these changes and show how they outweigh any of the potential benefits of the government plan.

The above example includes the internal link, which may or may not be used, depending on the debater.

It is smart to prepare as many disadvantages as possible in a policy case, and the depth of research that can tie the internal link to the plan is key to creating strong positions. Remember, the Opposition Team does not usually know the exact plan that will be argued by the Government Team, so there are usually disadvantages prepared on multiple potential interpretations.

Counterplans

Some debaters and coaches would argue that one of the main goals of policy interpretations is to mirror the act of passing legislation to fix real world problems. If this is the case, then there are many different ideas that need to be taken into account. What if this plan causes more problems than it fixes? This question was addressed with disadvantages. What if there is a better solution? This is a very interesting question, and it makes sense that if there is a better solution to the problem, then that solution should be preferred. This section will discuss what the opposition should do if they can come up with a better solution to solve for the problem.

Consider this for a moment. California has a bill to legalize marijuana. The bill is kicked around for a few months, and it basically legalizes marijuana for everyone in the state because they say it is the only solution to solve for the state debt. There is another group who also supports the legalization of marijuana, but they believe that it should be legal only for people over 21. They cite the potential for abuse at an early age as being a horrible possibility for the original bill, so they propose a different solution that would still fix the original problem. This would be an example of a counterplan.

Here are the main ideas: First, it needs to solve the problem better than the plan introduced by the government. Second, it should solve better than if the counterplan and plan were done at the same time. Third, it must have a specific text, with a mandate, agent, enforcement, and funding. Fourth, the plan must be competitive, meaning that it must force a choice between the plan and counterplan. There can be many reasons that a counterplan could be competitive. The most common reason is mutual exclusivity, meaning that it is logically impossible to do the counterplan and the plan at the same time. Another reason for competitiveness would look at the criterion, which is usually net benefits, and explain why the counterplan alone is better than the plan plus the counterplan.

The reason that the example marijuana counterplan can't be done in conjunction with the government plan is because the government plan specifies legality for everyone, while the opposition counterplan only allows for marijuana to be legal for individuals over 21. If it were to be done at the same time, it would involve language that made it both illegal and legal for individuals under 21. Either this makes no sense, or the government would have a host of issues on their hands by passing incoherent legislation.

The Difference between Debate and Reality in this Example

Debate has certain rules in order to preserve fairness for both sides, and one of those is that the Government Team shouldn't be able to change their original plan after it has been presented. In the above example, if there was a discussion and the only change to the original plan was to amend the age, both sides would probably agree and just change it in the original bill. However, since it wouldn't be fair if the Government Team could just change their plan whenever they wanted, they have to stick to their original proposal of legality for everyone. Notice that this is a change to their original plan, not adding on something that could be done at the same time. This concept will be discussed more in the following section on permutations.

Permutations

If the Government Team believes that the plan is not competitive, then they can "perm" the opposition counterplan. What this means is that if the counterplan does not force a choice between plan and counterplan, then the government is able to do both at the same time. When a counterplan is permed, the Government Team is not changing their original plan, merely adding the counterplan to it.

Perm Burdens

Currently most senior level debaters would agree that permutation of a counterplan does not necessarily require advocacy of that counterplan. If the judge believes that perms can be used as a test of competitiveness and not an addition to the government plan, then it makes sense for the Government Team to perm all counterplans. If the judge is on the fence or believes that perms are an additional advocacy to the government plan (rare), then Government Teams should be careful with perms and only use them when they truly believe that the counterplan and the plan working together is the best solution to the original problem.

The Issue of Non-topicality in Counterplans

In a policy debate, the resolution does not explicitly state a plan. In addition to coming up with definitions, the Government Team has the freedom to pick any plan they want as long as it falls under the scope of the topic. However, when the Government Team decides to present a plan, they are essentially providing an example/proposal that is a specific reason to support the resolution. For example: If the resolution is: This house should change its locks. The Government Team decides that this house is the USFG, should implies action, and change its locks means tighten border security. Then they propose a plan that says that the US Border Patrol will increase its workforce by 20%. Notice how all of this becomes more and more specific until the plan is actually discussed. Therefore, the plan is actually a form of defining the resolution.

If we can agree that the plan is a way of defining the resolution, then we have an interesting view of non-topicality and counterplans. One of the standard responses that many debaters provide when looking at the needs of counterplans is that they must be competitive and non-topical. If the plan is viewed as a level of specificity in the definitions, then it becomes the essence of the topic, and anything that is not plan then becomes non-topical. Therefore, all counterplans are non-topical because of the fact that they are not the government plan.

Formats

<u>Counterplan Title (brief 1-3 word title)</u>
<u>Plan text (or mandate)</u>
<u>Agent</u>
<u>Funding</u>
<u>Enforcement</u>

<u>Competitiveness</u>- Explain how the counterplan forces a choice between plan and counterplan

Non-Topical- Explain how plan is the embodiment of topicality, and therefore anything that is not-plan is therefore non-topical

Net Benefits- Explain how the counterplan solves for the problem better than the plan. This can be done in a couple of ways. Does it avoid a disadvantage? Does it create a large advantage that the plan can't accrue? You may want to even create separate counterplan advantages here. They would look like the advantages in the comparative advantages format of the government case.

Counterplan Dispositionality and Conditionality

When you bring a counterplan into a debate as the Opposition Team, you are introducing three options for the judge to vote for: the plan (if you lose), counterplan (if you win), or status quo (if plan causes more harm than doing nothing or counterplan, and you win on opp). Originally the ground of the status quo belonged to the opposition, however, the opp team can give this up to simply have the judge weigh plan vs. counterplan. This would be done by stating that the counterplan is *unconditional*. So at the end of the debate it is plan vs. counterplan, whoever can convince the judge their solution is better should win.

The second option would be to state that the counterplan is *dispositional*. What this means is that the opposition can get rid of the counterplan at any time, like a disadvantage, and not lose the debate. In this option they are still able to defend the status quo.

The third option is to claim that the counterplan is *conditional*. What this means is that the counterplan is simply a test of the resolution, and they can keep it or get rid of it. Debaters who claim this position also claims that disadvantages that link to both the plan and the counterplan are okay even though they are a contradiction of positions.

Generally the opp wouldn't want to run a disadvantage that links to both to their counterplan and the plan if they were running an unconditional counterplan, since this just evens out the impact on both sides. For example, with the plan to increase border patrol agents by 20%. Let's say that the Opposition Team runs a counterplan to increase border patrol agents by 25%. In addition, they are running a disadvantage that says increasing border patrol increases abuses of innocent civilians living in border towns. This disad would link to both, so if the Opposition Team was committed to keeping their counterplan then this disadvantage would equally impact both sides. If they could potentially get rid of the counterplan, then the disadvantages would still be relevant if there was no counterplan in the round.

Common Types of Counterplans

Study Counterplan- Study the problem more, and then do the plan

Consult Counterplan- Consult someone else (another country, NGO, whatever), and then do plan

Agent Counterplan- Do the plan but have someone else do it.

Exclusionary Counterplan- Do the plan but don't do a certain part of the plan

Something else that solves better for the problem counterplan- Do something else that solves the problem better.

A Few Things to Think About with Each Common Counterplan

Study Counterplan- You have to show that there is

currently not enough information to act right now. You have to show how acting right now would be bad and have a disadvantage tied to immediate non-study action.

Consult Counterplan- You have to show how talking to some other group first would make the plan solve better. Ideally have a disad that shows how no consultation would result in negative impacts.

Agent Counterplan- You have to show how your agent solves better. How does China doing the plan work better than the US doing the plan? You usually need to have agent specific disads that don't link to the counterplan agent.

Exclusionary Counterplan- You have to show how the one or two things that you are not including from the original plan link to your disadvantages.

Something else that solves better for the problem counterplan- This can really be anything to fix what the government is claiming to be an issue. The main burden it has to fulfill is to solve better than the government plan.

Remember- Since we are considering plans to be the essence of what is topical, and each of these examples are definitely not the government plan, then they are non-topical. In addition, each of these has the burden to show how they solve better than the plan in order for the Opposition Team to win with them.

Vagueness & Spec Arguments

The appropriate level of detail that parliamentary debaters need to explain is often up for question. How much of the plan should they describe? If they say that the agent is the United States Federal Government, is that enough? Most debaters believe that it is not, and that the Government Team should at least explain which branch of government will be enacting the plan. So let's say they have decided that congress will enact the plan. Is this specific enough? What if they have congress pass the plan, but they don't say how many votes are cast and who voted against it? Most debaters would agree that this level of detail is not necessary, but the argument that some vagueness is okay while others is not can often become confusing and make specification arguments difficult to provide brightline analysis as to what is not specific enough and what is sufficient. However, certain specifics should usually be provided, and if they are not, debaters should use the following tools to illustrate why specificity is important. The argument is formed in the same way as a topicality violation.

<u>Interpretation</u>
<u>Violation</u>
<u>Standards</u>
<u>Voting Issue/Impact</u>

In the <u>interpretation</u> step, you describe what you believe plans should look like. If the agent is in question here, you describe what level of detail the government needs to meet when discussing who is doing the plan in order to be adequate.

The <u>violation</u> discusses how they are not meeting that level of detail.

The <u>standards</u> discuss how this hurts debate. Usually Ground and another standard are used here.

The <u>voting issue or impact</u> discusses how this is to be weighed in the round. Usually a vague agent is not enough

do be an independent reason to vote down a Government Team. The opposition could discuss how vague agents hurt debate, which hurts the fairness of debate and will eventually force the activity into extinction. Another approach would be to discuss how passing legislation with vague parameters would lead to abuse of that legislation because of the loopholes the lack of specificity creates. Basically here the Opposition Team needs to illustrate clear reasons why vagueness is bad and explain how these reasons should be weighed against the other impacts in the debate.

ASPEC= Specification of the agent
ESPEC= Specification of enforcement
FSPEC= Specification of funding (almost never used)

Kritiks (also known as critiques, also known as "K")

Any time a team advocates for a certain position; whether it be their criterion, their definitions, their plan, their disadvantage, anything at all; they are justifying their arguments with certain philosophical beliefs. For example, if the Government Team advocates the use of the military to solve a crisis, they are coming from the philosophical belief that the use of force can be used to create peace. Another example could be that if the Government Team passes their plan through the US legislative branch, they are reinforcing the two party system.

What a Kritik does is it looks to the underlying assumptions of any action and extrapolates how these assumptions can lead to certain behaviors and impacts in other situations.

While the format of Kritiks can vary, one of the most easy to follow looks like a disadvantage with philosophy and background in the place of the description of a situation. For example:

<u>Philosophical Background</u>
<u>Link</u>
<u>Impact</u>

Certain debate scholars believe that there needs to be an alternative presented after the impact. In other words, there needs to be a different course of action for the debaters to take in order to avoid this Kritik. In some cases, it is like a philosophical counterplan, with a text that should be included and advocated. In other cases, the alternative is "reject the Government Team." We believe, that at least in parliamentary debate, kritiks function much better as a quasi-disadvantage than anything else.

Types of Kritiks

"They said_____"
This kritik looks at the language used by the opposing team. It can be run by government or opposition, and looks at linguistic choices made by each team. For example, if the Opposition Team continually refers to adult women as "girls," this kritik would discuss how this terminology reduces the worth of women to children and considers them less valuable members of society. There is a significant body of literature that could endorse this claim.

<u>Militarism K</u>
Any act that uses military force is bad. This would draw upon philosophies that reject force as a way of solving problems and advocate non-violent means. If the plan uses military action, this would then link to all of the

negative consequences of violence.

Capitalism K

Any plan that uses a capitalist system endorses capitalism. Capitalism is bad, they make it stronger, and here are a bunch of reasons why cap is bad.

A million other K's

Basically any philosophy can work as long as it can show some type of impact and can link to the plan or any language used in the round.

5 REBUTTALS

So far we have discussed arguments to be introduced in the first four speeches. We covered case construction on the government side for fact, value, and policy, and we also introduced responses to these cases and unique ways of arguing for the opposition. At the end of the debate there are two rebuttal speeches, one for the government, and one for the opposition. This chapter is intended to introduce the basic concepts behind these speeches.

In the first chapter, the speech names and orders were presented.
PMC
LOC
MGC
MOC
LOR
PMR

Opposition Rebuttals

As you may have noticed, the MOC (Member of Opposition Constructive) and LOR (Leader of Opposition Rebuttal) are two consecutive opposition speeches. This is a significant advantage late in the debate for the Opposition Team, since they have the opportunity to speak for twelve minutes straight (8 minutes for the MOC, 4 minutes for the LOR). When first encountering this format, many debaters ask the question- "So what, am I just supposed to repeat what my partner said in the rebuttal since I am not responding to anything?" The answer: yes and no. You are definitely not repeating any arguments word for word and with as much detail as in any of the constructive speeches. Your job is to find the best arguments, and put them together in an organized and easily understood format so your judge can see the debate clearly. Some coaches refer to this as "crystallization." Here are a few strategies for the Leader of Opposition Rebuttal Speech.

Strategy 1- Topicality First

If you decided to go for topicality all the way though the debate, then this issue should be raised first. Your arguments should have illustrated that topicality is something that should be voted upon before the rest of the debate, so because of this fact it should come first.

Strategy 2- Novice Debaters- Best arguments first

If you are new to parliamentary debate, always put your best arguments first (unless you are going for T, which will always go first). The main reason for this is time allocation. If you aren't absolutely sure that you will have time to get to every voting issue, then you need to absolutely cover the most important ones first.

Experienced Debaters- Primacy & Recency

Put your best arguments first and last. Communication research has shown that people tend to best remember the first thing and the last thing out of a speakers mouth. Because of this phenomenon, it follows that debaters should put their best arguments first and last and have their mediocre arguments in the middle.

Strategy 3 Revisit the Criterion

Early in the debate, a criterion was most likely agreed on. Whether it was net benefits, on balance, or something else, if it was agreed on, it is the lens that the judge is supposed to be weighing the arguments through. By re-introducing and focusing on the criterion your arguments are made clearer to the judge.

Strategy 4 Use Big Labels

Be very clear which arguments are most important and which ones you are clearly winning. You can label them "Voter number one, voter number two, voter number three," and so on, or you can simply label them by the name of the argument itself. However, if you label the argument by its original name, be very, very clear that you are starting with a separate reason to vote for your team.

Strategy 5- Don't Go for Everything

Now is the time to cut the fat. Get rid of the arguments that you know you are losing, and present to the judge exactly why you have been the stronger debate team. Teams that go for everything often end up making average arguments look just as important as arguments that clearly win the round. Clarity is everything for a judge.

Government Rebuttals

The prime minister delivers the final speech of the debate. The prime minister has a significant amount of information to cover. Not only does he or she have just five minutes to respond to an eight-minute constructive speech, but this speaker also has to respond to the four-minute rebuttal. In other words, this speaker has to cover and refute twelve minutes of arguments in a five-minute span. This inherent unbalance is one of the reasons that new arguments are not allowed during rebuttals.

A Few Strategies for Prime Minister Rebuttals

Strategy 1 Respond to the MOC

Be sure to respond to new arguments presented in the Member of Opposition Constructive speech. Since the MOC speech does allow new arguments, the PM has the ability to respond to these and refute them. While most teams will not, and usually should not, bring in big new arguments during their second constructive, they sometimes do. The PM should be sure to answer these first.

Strategy 2 Voter Turns

If you can take the opposition arguments and prove how they are actually arguments for the government, this puts you in a very strong position.

Strategy 3 Your Own Voters/Reasons to vote for your team

After you have directly responded to everything that needs to be covered, present your own voters. You may have turns that ended up being voters for your side already, but here you can present other separate reasons to vote for your team.

Strategy 4 Use the Criterion

Similar to the opp strategy discussed before, it is always beneficial to show the judge exactly how the arguments should be weighed. Your criterion was originally presented to do just this, so be sure to examine all arguments through this filter.

Strategy 5 Time Management

As discussed earlier, you have five minutes to answer 12 minutes of arguments. Be very aware of your time. The last thing you want to do is spend too much time answering their arguments and then not get to some key offensive points.

Overall the purpose of a rebuttal is to take the arguments that have been put out on the table and clarify them so the judge has an easier time evaluating the debate. As mentioned in chapter one, debaters should not introduce new arguments here, but they can elaborate on existing arguments. If this rule is violated, teams can raise a point of order.

STRATEGIC ARGUMENTATION IN PARLIAMENTARY DEBATE

6 GOVERNMENT RESPONSES TO OPPOSITION CASES

In Chapter Four we discussed many different tools that the opposition can use when arguing against the government. This chapter is intended to provide ways to articulate responses to these arguments.

Responses to Topicality

There are a few different ways to deal with T. Remember, the idea behind topicality is that the Government Team is being accused of defining the resolution in a way that is unfair to the Opposition Team. The argument provides analysis as to what the topic should have been, it explains how the Government Team did not meet this burden, it shows standards that definitions should uphold, and provides reasons why this should be an independent voting issue. The following responses are a few common ways that topicality is dealt with.

Response #1 to Topicality: "We meet."

What this response means is that the Government Team upholds the burden that the opposition is claiming that they violate. For example, let's say the topic was "If you like it then you should have put a ring on it," and the Government Team interpreted the topic as "If you like it," as if the United States Federal Government believes in equality, and "then you should have put a ring on it," as then they should pass legislation allowing for gay marriage in all states. If the Opposition Team was to try and run topicality, and their interpretation of the resolution is that "this implies bringing together two things that were once separate," the Government Team could argue against this with the "we meet" argument. They would say that they are in fact brining together two things that were once separate, gays and marriage or two once separate individuals into one union, this would then make them topical under the interpretation provided by the opposition.

Response #2 to Topicality: Argument Turns

This strategy includes taking the standards and voters that have already been used by the Government Team and showing how your definition is actually fairer under these parameters. For example, if the Opposition Team argues that they have lost ground in the debate, the Government Team would argue that their interpretation actually allows for *more ground* than the opposition would have under their own interpretation. This basically turns their argument against the Opposition Team. We recommend this strategy simply because it garners the most impacts in the least amount of time.

Response #3 Counter Standards & Counter Voters

Remember, the Government Team must argue against all parts of topicality introduced by the opposition. In this strategy, they discuss all of the elements of the topicality argument presented by the opposition, and also introduce counter standards and counter voters. Counter standards are reasons why the Government Team's definitions are superior to those provided by the opposition. For example, if the Opposition Team uses the standard of *predictability*, and explains how the definitions given by the government are completely unpredictable and therefore unfair, the Government Team could provide the counter standard of *creativity*. They would explain that creativity is something to be valued, and the purposeful ambiguity inherent in some topics allows for this creative liberty to thrive and leads to productive and innovative debates. Overall, counter standards are similar to regular standards; the main difference is that they endorse the definitions given by the Government Team as a way of refuting topicality.

Counter voters function in a similar way to counter standards. If the Opposition Team argues a counter voter of fairness, the government could argue the counter voter of jurisdiction, explaining that definitions don't necessarily need to be completely fair, but that they just need to be within the scope of what the judge can rule on. Due to time constraints, turns are used more often than counter positions when dealing with topicality.

Responses to Disadvantages

The next section discusses common answers to disadvantages. In earlier chapters we explained how disadvantages address problems that the plan can create. We covered the possible formats and discussed the terms:

status quo, uniqueness, link, internal link, and impact. This section will look at the internal components of disadvantages and common ways to argue against them.

Non-Unique

Uniqueness is the idea that the situation will only be only effected by the government plan, and it will not happen on its own. One common response to disadvantages is that the problem is "non-unique." This claim means that the problem will happen anyways, regardless of whether or not plan is passed.

No Link

The second approach to answering disadvantages is that there is no link. It is the job of the opposition to clearly illustrate how the plan will cause the impact. This strategy is designed to question whether or not the plan will lead to the impact. In cases where there is no internal link analysis, this is often a good approach. In other words, does the plan *really* effect the status quo, and does that effect *really* lead to the impact?

Impact Turn

The third approach to answer a disadvantage closely examines the impact. This is referred to an impact turn. The main idea here is that the impact that the opposition is claiming to be bad is actually good. For example, if the Opposition Team claims that the disadvantage will lead to the destruction of the finance industry, the Government Team would argue that this destruction is the only possible route to fix the problem and that it is actually a good thing in the long run. Overall, debaters using this strategy argue that the impacts of a disadvantage that the opposition believes to be bad are actually good.

Threshold

The last approach to responding to disadvantages looks at the amount of change that needs to happen before the impacts occur. When the Opposition Team provides a disadvantage, they have the burden to show that the situation is on the brink of change, and that the plan is enough change to push it into the impact. If they don't show how much change is needed, then they are not providing enough "threshold" to meet this burden. For example, if the status quo is the number six, and the plan adds one, and the Opposition Team can show that when the status quo hits seven it will change and lead to the impact. If the Opposition Team can't show exactly when the impact will occur, then the Government Team should be able to take this argument apart.

Often times your response will be a response to a response. For example, you say that your plan will increase financial success in the US. The opp says that greed is the root of the problem, and it will lead to taking advantage of people in 3rd world countries. The response to this would be to defend this taking advantage, and explain how your plan doesn't directly increase this and overall is net beneficial. This is just the use of four-point refutation on the government side. Four-point refutation is used in many situations as a direct response. Sometimes this can be used to mitigate an argument and make it ineffective, but other times, when a turn is implemented, it can actually garner more offense for the Government Team.

Responses to Kritiks

As mentioned earlier, Kritiks use philosophical implications as a means for explaining how certain mentalities effect the status quo. Similar to a disadvantage, each part of a kritik can be attacked.

Philosophy

If the philosophy is somehow misunderstood this is a great opportunity to explain the correct interpretation. After the correct interpretation is discussed, this should be elaborated on in order to show the positive impact of the plan.

Link

Here you might be able to show that the plan doesn't exactly link to the philosophy. You can illustrate how other factors are at play, and your plan isn't a pure example of that particular philosophy, therefore the implications of the mindset aren't accurate. Also, sometimes you can show how teams actually link into their own Kritik.

Impact Turn

The things that the Kritik causes to happen are actually good.

7 FLOWING

One of the most important skills in advanced debate is your ability to take accurate notes. This is referred to as <u>flowing</u>. Your notes are referred to as your "flow." Some coaches advocate a novice style to get started and another format for more advanced debaters; we believe that the advanced style allows for all students to learn faster and stay more organized. However, both styles will be discussed so students can decide which they feel will work best.

Style 1 (Novice)

Using blank computer paper, turn the page horizontally.

Draw five equally spaced lines on your paper, which should create six separate columns.

At top of each column, write the name of the speech.
The speeches should be as follows: PMC, LOC, MGC, MOC, LOR, PMR

Style 2 (Advanced)

The second and preferred way for flowing is as follows:

Keep each position on a different sheet of paper.

"Positions" include Case (what is said in the PMC), each disadvantage, K's, Topicality, or any other large argument.

Label each position at the top of the page.

Practice!!!

Be sure to abbreviate words. Make sure you get each label, such as link, brink, impact, A, B, C, etc. The purpose of the labels is to allow students to keep track of large amounts of information.

Pens?

We recommend using two pens, one color for opposition and one color for government. This allows you to quickly see which side said what.

The best way to get better at flowing is to PRACTICE!

8 GOVERNMENT STRATEGIES

Now that we have covered the basics, it is time to explore some of the more innovative strategies that teams use in advanced debates.

Pre-Fiat Impacts

It is rare to ever see pre-fiat impacts in a novice round. The main idea behind this perspective is that the only thing that we are really doing is talking, and the talk that we engage in is the only true impact. If pre-fiat impacts are the main impacts being introduced and weighed by the Government Team, then they will likely make the argument that fiat is an illusion and that the plans that we argue don't really do anything. All of this needs to be discussed in a framework argument. Here is a bullet point example of the framework of a case that focuses on pre-fiat implications.

- Discourse and language create reality (needs detailed explanation)
- Our case presents an issue that educates people in round about X

- By talking about X, we get these impacts in round

This type of argument is predicated on discourse. It looks at the idea that we are just people in a room talking back and forth. There is no actual plan that gets passed. There are no impacts on poverty, nothing that effects our financial system, and all of the alleged impacts are just part of a game. However, the way we talk about issues and the language that we use to make examples will continue after the round. For example, if sexist language were used in a debate round, the argument would follow that not rejecting the team who uses this language creates a mindset that will lead to sexist behaviors outside of the round.

These types of arguments can also be used to embrace new ways of thinking. For example, in one of the elimination rounds of NPDA in 2009, a team proposed a policy case that didn't give a plan. They said, "it was a secret." They argued that parli debate has become too entrenched in fiat and that it doesn't really do anything, so their rejecting of plans created an idea virus that would lead to actual change and education, rather than hypothetical change through fiat.

Vague to Specific

Parliamentary debate often has very vague resolutions. Sometimes they are metaphors, and sometimes they are simply just vague. At the senior levels, this usually gives a fairly large strategic advantage to the Government Team. In a metaphor, topicality usually goes out the window. The Government Team must still adhere to the relationships between the words, but the topic is pretty much up for grabs. Government Teams should prepare cases in order to take advantage of this situation. They should be significant and appropriate, and should not be used to cheat. Since the Government Team has the option to discuss virtually any topic, it is smart to pick one that will give them the utmost advantage.

Is That Value is Really a Policy?

Often times many senior debaters will make every single topic a policy resolution. For those coaches and judges who believe that each resolution has a strict interpretation of fact, value, or policy, this can be very frustrating. However, especially in the Midwest and on the East Coast, this has become extremely common. It is rare that students argue that a policy resolution should be interpreted as a value, or that any resolution should be argued as a fact. An example framework that supports viewing all resolutions as a policy is as follows:

-    Policy rounds test how the philosophical and hypothetical nature of the resolution would materialize
- Plans offer more ground to both sides
-    Policy debate is more real world, and it allows for better education for future   policy-making

So even a resolution like, "Healthcare is more important than national security,"
could have teams that propose a plan that solves for health care, claiming that if health care is more important than national security, then we should do something about it. Teams like this would claim that all this resolution does is beg for support of health care plans because of its importance.

Some teams believe that every resolution can be interpreted as a policy. These teams often do very well. The adherence to the interpretation of resolutions as facts, values, or policies is up to each individual debate team and coach preference.

STRATEGIC ARGUMENTATION IN PARLIAMENTARY
DEBATE

9 OPPOSITION STRATEGIES

The role of the opposition can be very challenging. "If I don't know how they are going to interpret the topic, how can I prepare?" This chapter is intended to provide some concrete planning strategies for the Opposition Team that include time allocation, order of preparation, and a few other small tricks.

Prepare Topicality First

When the Opposition Team first hears the topic, their main job is to understand what possible interpretations the government could run. Not only does this first step involve figuring out what the Government Team might do, but it also involves figuring out what they shouldn't be allowed to do. As we have discussed in previous chapters, certain topics have more leeway than others, but there are always limitations on each topic. Therefore, the first thing that the Opposition Team should prep is topicality. This might take a few minutes, or it might take only a few seconds. Here is an example of a topic that would only take a few seconds: "California should vote yes on proposition 8." Why does this one only take a few seconds? Because there really aren't too many ways that you can twist this topic. The only potential ambiguity would be proposition 8. A savvy Government Team might try to stretch this and find an older proposition 8 that may have not been voted on in the past. However, most teams will interpret his resolution straight up and be predictable.

At NPDA nationals in 2008, one of the topics was "Silence the red phone." There are a few potential interpretations here: eliminate the red phone contact with the White House and Russia or ban the commercials run by Hillary Clinton that had recently run that featured a red cell phone. If the Opposition Team believes that these are the only two legitimate possibilities, then they should be prepared to run topicality if the interpretation is anything else. In fact, when there is a topic where it seems like there should truly only be a couple separate interpretations, these two ways of redefining the topic can be explained in the first section of the topicality violation. The opp would explain- it should be either A, or B. Everything else is unfair.

Prepare Disadvantages After Topicality

Since the topicality preparation is defined to gain an understanding of the different legitimate interpretations, this then should allow the Opposition Team to have a much better idea of the plans that will be run. Because the opposition has now decided which interpretations they will defend, they should now be ready to create disadvantages.

The opposition should create as many disadvantages as possible. They should be sure to create them for any interpretation that they believe is legitimate.

Create More Generic Positions after Disadvantages

The next step would to create disadvantages or kritiks

that link to very general concepts inherent in the resolution. These positions are intended to still link to the resolution if the Government Team hits you with some type of interpretation that still makes sense but you really didn't think of it. This would include arguments like militarism K's, capitalism K's, or an economy/funding disadvantage.

So overall, the best way the Opposition Team can prepare is to first prepare topicality to see what they will need to argue against, then create specific arguments against the topics they believe that they will need to debate, and last create general positions that they believe will link to pretty much every possible interpretation.

10 JUDGING

There are different skill levels of debate, and different expectations of judges at each level. At the senior level, the judges should have senior experience or a bachelor's degree. At the rookie level, judges need to be...not a rookie. At the end of the day the main idea is that the judge should vote for the team who had the most convincing arguments. This is a very difficult concept to pin down. At most national tournaments, senior level judges are required to submit a judging philosophy due to the differing perspectives on what makes the most convincing arguments. Since NPDA requires the following questions to be answered in a judge's philosophy, let's look at these first to understand differing judge perspectives:

How many parli rounds have you judged this year?
How many non-parli rounds have you judged this year?
What is you decision-making approach?
How do you assess arguments?
Do you have presentational preferences?
Do you have any particularly strong viewpoints on certain issues?

How do you feel about cases, DA's, K'S, T, etc.?
Other items to note?

These are what NPDA feels should be the bare bones of a judging philosophy. In other words, judges should have opinions about each of these areas before evaluating a debate at the national level.
Challenges

No matter which way you vote, there are usually at least some redeeming points on each side of the debate, especially in in advanced rounds. Here are a few tools to guide you:

Learn to flow. Effective note taking is crucial to making an effective decision.

Have a firm judging philosophy. If you know where you stand on certain controversial issues, it is easier to sign a ballot for one team over another.

How to Write a Ballot

The spaz. Write everything that comes to mind that could have potentially influenced you.

The plus & RFD- Draw a plus on your ballot. Make each square specific to each speaker and write comments regarding each speech. Write the RFD, or reason for decision at the very bottom below the plus.

The rebuttal recap- Since rebuttals are the main arguments that the debaters are going for, some judges choose to write comments on the issues discussed in the rebuttal. After these issues are weighed, the judge will write a reason for the decision.

How to Handle Points of Order

Earlier in the book, points of order were discussed as a

way of interrupting speakers if a new argument is presented in a rebuttal speech. The judge has three options when a student raises a point of order.

Point well taken- This response means that the judge agrees that the argument is new and the team who brought in the argument needs to stop that particular point.

Point not well taken- This response means that the judge does not agree that it is a new argument and the speaking team can proceed with what they were discussing earlier.

Point taken under consideration- This means that either it doesn't matter, or the judge will think about it. This is the stock response whenever there is more than one judge.

Overview

Judging debates can be very rewarding and fun. It is very challenging but gives the critic a great opportunity to sharpen his or her analytic skills.

11 RESEARCH

Although some teams may attend a tournament with no evidence whatsoever and compete in parliamentary debate, almost all senior teams would argue that this is not a smart strategy. It can be said that parliamentary debate knowledge is understanding a little bit about everything, rather than everything about one subject. Also, because debaters only have 20 minutes from the time that a topic is announced to prepare their case and make their way to the room they are competing in, research should be easily digestible. This chapter provides structures for briefs on specific issues and common topics.

Specific Issues Briefs

Current events need to be understood since almost all tournaments have at least one topic that focuses specifically on them. We recommend the following brief structure:

Summary

Discuss the overall issue, include background, key players, current developments.

STRATEGIC ARGUMENTATION IN PARLIAMENTARY DEBATE

Pro
What is going well with the issue, how is it being resolved or made better than it was in the past?

Con
What is going wrong with this issue, how is it getting worse?

Plans
Has anyone developed a solution or proposal to make a significant change to the issue? If so, what are the details on these plans?

Common Topic Briefs

This type of brief includes details on some issues that frequently come up. Topics could include:

Military Action Good/Bad
Capitalism Good/Bad
More Government Control Good/Bad
Socialism Good/Bad

Each of these could be formatted as follows:

Brief topic: _____

Pro Examples
Discuss current examples of the issue that support your argument

Pro Theories
Discuss theories and commentary that supports your argument

Con Examples
Discuss examples of the issue that oppose the

argument

Con Theories
Discuss theories and commentary that opposes the argument

Be Familiar With Your Research
There is no substitute for having read the research before the debate round. Only so much can be done during prep time, and the more debaters know outside of prep, the better equipped they will be to compete.

12 ARGUMENTATION STRATEGIES AND LOGICAL FALLACIES

While there are many different ways in which people can approach arguments, there are a few common strategies that come up time after time. This chapter is intended to discuss these techniques and their application to parliamentary debate. Students often remember the six main argument strategies through the acronym GASCAP.

GASCAP

Generalization
Analogy
Sign
Causal
Authority
Principle

Argument from Generalization

Individuals who use this strategy are claiming that what is true of a well represented sample is true for the whole population. Examples of this would include: polls, detailed case studies, and any type of sampling where the entire population is not used. In parliamentary debate, this is a very common way of using small pieces of data to generalize how an entire population feels or how a population will act.

Argument from Analogy

This type of argument is one of the foundational ways that our courts function in the United States. If a court case is similar to another new case in important ways, it can be used as a precedent. The more relevant similarities, the stronger the analogy. Arguments from analogy look at two separate cases, and use their similarities in order to make conclusions. This is often seen in solvency arguments, because the debater is trying to show how "if it worked in instance X, it will work in instance Y."

Argument from Sign

This type of argument evaluates the symptoms as a way to figure out the disease. For example, if a student were to smell like alcohol and have a stamp on their wrist that looked like they just came from the campus bar, we could make the case that they had been drinking. Similar to the argument from analogy, the relevance of signs as well as the number of signs strengthens this argument. Debaters often see this type of argument when they are describing impacts.

Causal Argument

Notice that this word is causal, as in cause and effect, not casual, as in "informal." This type of argument examines situations that almost always occur together and links them. In some cases, the relationship has occurred so many times that we consider it a scientific law, such as the effect of a ball falling to the floor when you release it out of your hand. In this case, one thing always preceded the other with such frequency and reliability that there was no longer a question of whether or not it was true. However, in cases where human behavior or the results of policies are concerned, it is much more difficult to clearly attribute causes.

Argument from Authority

This is just like it sounds. I am an expert, I say that it is true, therefore, it is true. This particular argument relies heavily on the credibility of the source, and is strengthened by the recognized credibility indicators the source can provide. For example, is the source an M.D., a PhD? Does this person have come from a relatively non-biased group? In parliamentary debate, the use of authority is different than other types of debate because there is no truly reliable source data within the round since everything is handwritten during prep time. However, the names of certain news organizations, philosophers, and scholars are often used to gain argument credibility.

Argument from Principle

Killing people is wrong, therefore, I shouldn't kill anyone. This argumentative strategy looks at commonly accepted principles and uses them as a means to make determinations in specific instances. However, it is very challenging to find principles that have no exceptions. For example, in the above statement that "killing is wrong," most people believe that killing is not wrong in all instances. Is killing wrong in war to stop torture of innocent civilians? Is killing wrong to save your family? Principles can be unpacked at various levels by debaters, but are often used as a justification for impacts. The reason most impacts involve death, dehumanization, torture, poverty, and things like this is because debaters generally believe that the judge will agree with the principle that it is wrong to kill, dehumanize, torture, etc.

Logical Fallacies

This next portion of this chapter is intended to examine logical fallacies that can be seen through the misuse of the previously discussed strategies as well as a few other ways that arguments sometimes mask or divert attention from the issue being discussed. A logical fallacy is an error in reasoning or logic that can lead receivers to inaccurate conclusions. There are many possible logical fallacies, and the following section identifies some of the most common.

Straw Man

This argument presents your opponents weakest argument as if it were the strongest. In debate you may see this as a way to focus away from issues you may not be winning as a diversionary tactic.

Non Sequitur

This logical fallacy makes claims that do not logically follow one another. For example, "John is rich and he just bought a new car. His car must be expensive." Notice here how in the first claim we know nothing about John's spending habits or whether or not he likes cars. All we know is that he is rich. Therefore, the next claim that is made is made on insufficient grounds and does not logically follow the first statement.

Appeal to Ignorance

This logical fallacy argues that because something has not been proven false, then it must be true. For example, a teacher might foolishly say, "Since I didn't catch anyone cheating on the test, then obviously no one cheated." While this example illustrates this concept clearly, it can be found in much more complicated arguments.

Argumentum Ad Populum

Argumentum ad populum assumes that if something is popular, then it must be good, right and/or true. It is used often when justifying the policies of popular political figures that were democratically elected or any type of popular trends.

Post Hoc Ergo Propter Hoc

Literally this is translated as *after this, therefore, because of this*. Essentially it means is that since this thing has happened, and this other thing happened before it, the thing that happened first must have caused it. For example, I walked into the room wearing pants, and everyone left. Everyone must have left because I was wearing pants. Notice how these two things happened in sequence, however, one did not necessarily cause the other. Instead they just followed each other in sequence.

Appeal to Inertia

This logical fallacy argues that because something has been a certain way for a long time, and it continues to be that way, then it must be right and good. Often times you will see this show up in solvency arguments in debate cases. This type of reasoning resists change and usually doesn't understand or justify the position it represents.

False Analogy

A false analogy compares two things that are not similar in relevant ways. Apples and oranges. For example, "Of course I am going to be a good new debater, I argue with my girlfriend all the time." Notice how this statement is trying to compare the quality of arguing with a girlfriend to the quality of arguing in debate. They sound somewhat similar on face value, but they are not similar enough to make it a sound argument.

False Dilemma

This logical fallacy provides two options as if they were the only two. Examples: Either you are with us or you are against us. Either you vote for the plan provided by the Government Team, or the US will be attacked with nuclear weapons.

Guilt or Glory by Association

This false logic associates certain ideas and concepts with something or someone who is already viewed positively or negatively by the message receiver. This false logic is the reason that advertisers use famous people to sell their products. It can also be a way to overlook questionable content of a message if the speaker is credible enough.

Slippery Slope

This will lead to this, and then this, and then this. A slippery slope fallacy is a chain of events that don't have adequate backing to be realistic. Advantages and disadvantages are often said to be slippery slopes, because they are arguments that sometimes justify grand effects that need a long sequence of events to actually happen.

Ad Hominem

Roughly translated as "against the man," this logical fallacy tricks the listener in order to make him or her examine speaker credibility rather than the argument itself. For example, when discussing the current governor of California, one might say, "How can you even look at his plans, he was the terminator." This argument is basically saying that since he was a movie star he is incapable of creating quality plans, rather than looking at the plans themselves to identify if they are good or not.

This is not an exhaustive list of logical fallacies. After reading this chapter, students should be able to identify shaky arguments in a debate round and apply four-point refutation. Second, debaters can also find times in history when these arguments have been passed off as facts, and link the endorsement of the same type of reasoning to the past negative consequences. Last, the ability to identify common logical problems makes individuals better consumers of information.

13 PRACTICE STRATEGIES

Debate Against the Computer

There are many different parliamentary debate rounds available on internet video websites.
http://net-benefits.net actively compiles a list of the available debate rounds. One strategy to gain experience debating against challenging opponents is to practice debating against the PMC speech of one of these videos. Practice responding to all of their arguments, and craft specific ways that you would attack their case.

Speed Overview

Speed is a huge factor in debate. While some believe that speed is the downfall of debate, others believe that the more arguments the better. Whether you like it or not, the top debaters have the ability to talk fast. Here are a few ways to get up to speed.

Become familiar with your positions.

Familiarity is the mother of speed. Most debaters can

present arguments that they know faster than those that they are just learning. This may sound like common sense, but this is probably the largest influencing factor on effective speed.

Good speed and bad speed.

Good speed presents arguments in digestible chunks. Bad speed doesn't stop, even for a second. It blends points together and is very confusing.
Good speed still sounds like a human. Bad speed takes gasps of air and sounds like an asthma attack.
Good speed emphasizes main points, provides vocal variety, and is conscious of what is being said. Bad speed is a robot, monotone, and says words rather than meaning.
Good speed develops arguments through detailed explanation. Bad speed dumps a bunch of bad arguments to force the other team to drop semi-important points.
Good speed can still make grandma understand and care about your arguments. Bad speed can only be understood by a debate coach with 10 years of experience.
Good speed makes your slower presentations better, easier, and more powerful. Bad speed makes your slower presentations feel awkward and like they are in slow motion.

Speed: Shorter Time, Same Debate

This activity involves doing the same debate twice. The first step is to have a debate in the normal fashion. Once the debate is finished, using the same notes and the same arguments, both teams should try and shorten their speeches by one minute each and still argue everything that was covered. This is an excellent way to illustrate how much faster most debaters can speak when they are familiar with a topic.

Speed: Pencil in the Mouth Drill

While this may feel silly, it is sort of like weight lifting for your mouth. Practice giving one of your constructive speeches with a pencil in your mouth. When you take the pencil out, it will feel like you can move your mouth much quicker and easier. This drill has mixed results.

Speed: Semi-Memorize

There should be blocks of information that you use that are virtually the same every time they come out of your mouth. Identify these and practice saying them over and over again. Some examples of the most common blocks of information that are used include:
Topicality Standards
Topicality Voters
Responses to Topicality Standards and Voters
Generic Disads
Certain Impacts, especially pre-fiat

More Preparation: Practice Case Construction

Don't debate, just create cases. This activity is extremely valuable to eliminate drag and figure out the roles of partners. Pick the five most likely topics that you could expect at the next tournaments, and create as many cases as possible for each topic. This exercise alone can lead to a significant boost in the winning percentage of any team.

14 FINAL THOUGHTS

Like any activity that utilizes performance, Parliamentary Debate is constantly changing. It is an activity that promotes critical thinking, advocacy, and the skills to significantly change our world. It becomes a process of learning how to think in a different way, and through this students are transformed. Whether you as the reader are a novice or an experienced debater, these skills will last, and we congratulate you taking such an important step.

Made in the USA
San Bernardino, CA
15 December 2018